# EPHESUS

# EPHESUS

## The civilisation of western Anatolia and a dazzling paradise of nature

### WHERE IS EPHESUS?

Ephesus is in the western part of Asia Minor, also called Anatolia, which today forms part of the Republic of Turkey. It is near the historical town of Selçuk (Seljuk), between the cities of Aydın and İzmir (Symrna). It is 6 km. from the Aegean Sea and 680 km. from Istanbul, 55 km. from Aydın, 225 km. from Denizli (Hierapolis), 180 km. from Bodrum, 205 km. from Marmaris and 510 km. from Antalya (please look at the map).

### HOW TO GET TO EPHESUS

You can get there from two directions.
1. It will take you about an hour if you travel by taxi from İzmir; the 74 km. is covered by an excellent road. Dolmuses or buses also

run there regularly. Ephesus itself is 4 km. from Selçuk. You can find transport from Selçuk at any time. On the way back to İzmir it is also easy to find a bus.

2. The second way is via Kuşadası (Scala Nova, or in very early times. Neo-Polis): Most of the trourists coming by ship to Turkey in order to visit Ephesus, first call at Kuşadası, a pleasant resort town on the shores of the Aegean. From there, a main road takes you the 19 km. to Ephesus.

## GENERAL INFORMATION ABOUT EPHESUS

The name of Ephesus does not only remind one of the city itself, but also calls to mind Artemis, St. John and the Church of St. Mary. The latter attracts the interest of Christians all over the world. However, these sites are some distance from each other. The distance between St. John and St. Mary for example, is about 10 km., and if you wish to see the monuments between them you should spend a whole day there. When you spend a night at Selçuk, you will not only be able to see the history and wonders of centuries past, as well as the House of the Virgin Mary (which was discovered through the vision of a pious Bohemian woman, but you will also enjoy the hospitality and customs of the Turkish people. Ephesus was built in the most beautiful part of Western Anatolia. You realize this as soon as you enter the city. In fact it is not difficult to imagine the historical past of the city, namely that of the Roman era, when Ephesus was the capital of five hundred Anatolian towns.

This was after the period in which Homer wrote his immortal works, and the time in which St. John lived and died. At that time you could see the stairs of the colossal theatre from the sea far away, and the huge gleaming columns of the Temple of Artemis, which once used to blind people with their beauty. About 250.000 people used to live in this famous city where the most skilful artisans and rich merchants gathered together. The entertainments held in honour of Artemis every year during April, were very gay. Spectators used to fill the theatres, which were an essential part of their lives. About a million people made up the audiences during

that special month. Sportsmen, musicians and theatre players used to attract people from the surrounding area, and spectators from as far away as Jerusalem and Athens as well. The great Temple of Artemis at Ephesus was one of the 7 wonders of the ancient world. The ruins of Ephesus are magnificent. Though hundreds of years have passed, and in spite of the ravages of time, they have survived to the present day, and even more than that, they still preserve their grace and elegance. After its decline. Ephesus was abandoned and forgotten for a long time. About a century ago the excavations of this ancient city began. Restoration has been undertaken continuously over the last ten years, so that some of this historical treasure, which had previously been buried for centuries, can now be seen and admired by millions.

## THE HISTORY OF EPHESUS

Ephesus was first constructed on a bay where the Küçük Menderes river (classical Kaystros) reached the sea in western Anatolia. This area is almost in the middle of ancient Ionia, which has a mild, wet climate, so that it has many natural advantages as a place for people to settle. It was not only situated at an important point joining the West and the East, but was also at the crossroads between Miletus and Ionia. The fine arts, the sciences, and philosophers such as Heraclitus and Thales, flourished and developed in Ionia. The cities of Ionia showed strong religious characteristics from the beginning, and became politically well-organised. Every city was self-governing. Ephesus has always been a city under two influences: The first geological, the second political, indeed it is difficult to separate these two influences from each other, and one has always been the cause of the other or the result of it. It is not certain who first founded Ephesus and when. Our first information about it comes from the year 2000 B.C., and its existence was mentioned near the temple of the mother goddess Kybele, a figure who was later called Artemis. The oldest sources record that the Amazons founded the town, and that it was then inhabited by the Carians and the Lelegians.

# IONIAN PERIOD IN EPHESUS

Ephesus was conquered by the Ionians in the 11th century. B.C. Androclos the son of Kadros from Athens, who was building a new town on the coast about one and a half kilometres from the temple, made his people settle there. This coastal town was a typical Ionian city, finely adorned with temples in honour of the Greek goddess and god Athena and Apollo. The Acropolis (the Byzantine fountain now stands in its stead on the small hill on the plan), which was almost completely destroyed, was located in front of the small round hill before the stadium. Until the 6th century, King Androclos governed the country in a semi-oligarchic fashion, and then up to the second half of the same century he ruled it as a tyrant. During the reign of Androclos, Ephesus maintained relations with the kings of Lydia, but the King of Lydia, Koressos, had the city surrounded, and forced the inhabitans to dwell on the plain, not far from the Temple of Artemis. At that period, the great philosopher, Heraclitus, who had a strong influence on ancient philosophy, lived here between the years 540-480 B.C. After the Persian Wars, a new era of democracy flourished in Ephesus and this Athenian method of rule was practised. During the Peloponnesian Wars, Ephesus first came under the domination of Athens and then Sparta (404 B.C.). After the Battle of Granikos in 334 B.C., Alexander the Great came to Ephesus and the city was won from the Persians. Later, one of the successors of Alexander the Great, named Lysimachos, conquered the city in

*General View*

the year 283 B.C.

As time passed, the plain became filled with sand carried by the Küçük Menderes river, and the direct outlet of the city to the sea was cut off. In addition, the plain became a marshy land which brought the city's inhabitants face to face with the danger of malaria. Lysimachos thought that a city located near such a marsh would be unsuitable for the inhabitants, both from a health point of view and from the point of view of commerce. To escape this unhealthy site, Lysimachos moved the city to a valley between Panayır mountain and Bulbul mountain, and in spite of great difficulties, he succeeded in this venture. This new area was more healthy and the city was better planned. Lysimachos encircled the city walls, the remains of which can still be seen today. He forced some of the people who didn't want to leave their old homes to move to the new city, by means of artificially flooding the old area using the water reservoir. He called the city after his wife, Arsinoe. At the same time, the city became one of the richest in the region and a centre for trade in ancient times. It was decorated with stadiums, gymnasiums and theatres, and continued to develop in the later Hellenistic and Roman periods, owing its continued existence to the forethought of Lysimachos.

## THE ROMAN PERIOD IN EPHESUS

After the death of Lysimachos, Ephesus was brought under the rule of Egypt and Syria. Then it was mastered by the Romans in the year 190 B.C. The Romans ruled Ephesus indirectly for a long time through Pergamum. At first, the people of Ephesus could not enjoy a peaceful life because of the wars around them, but they lived well later in the Augustan period (63 B.C.-14 A.D.). Soon Ephesus became the capital and also the most important commercial centre for the Roman province of Asia; the great writer of that age, Aristides, has told us this. Almost all religious, cultural and civic buildings, the remains of which are on the picture postcards you see today, belong to this period, when Ephesus was called the bank of Asia

minor. Those jubilant days ended in the year 3 A.D. It is very clear that the Goths who sacked the Temple of Artemis, had no mercy for Ephesus in their plundering. Later, Ephesus became the capital of Roman bishoprics of Asia Minor in the 4th century. The Third Council, one of the most important events in the history of Christianity, was held in the Church of St. Mary, with 200 bishops who were brought here at the command of Emperor Theodosius. The controversy about whether or not the Virgin Mary was the mother of Christ or of God, was discussed at this meeting in the 5th century.

## ARTEMIS

"Artemis of Ephesus is divine." The country of great Artemis, the goddess of hunting and the chase, stood around the bay of the Küçük Menderes river (kaystros). As time passed, the bay was filled with silt carried by the water of the river. In ancient times, before the Ionians, it is believed that a certain goddess of abundance ruled over the land. It is known that the old inhabitants of this country, that is, the Carians and the Lelegians, used to call the goddess of abundance whom they worshipped, "Great Mother". When we examine the culture of that age, we find the same goddess in a different guise. Though there is a big question as to what name she was called, we know that this goddess was worshipped. After the Ionians came to this city, they called the nameless goddess. Artemis, a Greek word. When the Ionians came to the bay of Küçük Menderes, between the two roads leading to the bay there stood a temple. This was surrounded with walls. In it there was a wooden statue representing Artemis the goddess. This was the first of many statues of Artemis and it was accepted as one of the 7 wonders of the ancient world. When Croesus, the King of the Lydians invaded this area, the temple was ruined, and so the king himself offered to build another temple of stone and presented some pillars to decorate the new Temple of Artemis. The temple site is now a ditch about one or two hundred metres on the righthand side of the road leading from Selçuk to Ephesus.

After Alexander the Great defeated the Persians in the year 334 B.C. he visited Ephesus, liked it very much and revered it. He organised a parade full of pomp in honour of the goddess. He promised the Ephesians that he would undertake all the expenses for Artemis, but the proud Ephesians declined this offer and smartly replied in such a way that even Alexander was pleased by the answer: "It would not befit a deity like you to build a temple to another deity". There was another reason for Alexander, who later received the title of "the Great" at the age of twenty, to feel such great reverence towards Artemis. When Alexander was born in Pella, the metropolis of Macedonia near Salonika in 356 B.C. the Temple of Artemis in Ephesus was burnt down that same night by a madman named Herostratus, who wished to become famous by doing this. On a question about this to the Ephesians: "Why couldn't your goddess protect her temple from destruction by fire?" it was answered: "Because our goddess had gone to Pella to be present at the birth of the Great Alexander."

Today, only a huge ditch remains from the majestic and colossal monument of that age. After this conflagration, the new temple was erected with the assistance of the most famous architects of the time, Praxiteles and Skopas, and decorated with statues. The statue of the goddess, ornamented with gold and brilliant marble, used to

blaze in the light.

As is mentioned above and as we read in some documents, the story of "Great Artemis of Ephesus" is explained as follows: In the early days of Christianity, a conflict had begun between the God of Christians and all the pagan gods. One of those who carried out this campaign was St. Paul. During that period a certain jeweller, Demetrius, used to make silver miniatures of the Temple of Artemis and sell them. He heard that St. Paul stated that idols made by man could not be gods and should not be sacred and worshipped. Demetrius explained this situation to the artisans who worked in his workshop. As a result these men, who believed deeply in Artemis and considered that their interests would be greatly endangered if the temple lost its importance, marched to the great theatre in a group shouting: "Great is Artemis of Ephesus." It became such a big crowd that most people hadn't any idea why they came together. This confusion was created by the artisans on purpose. Many orations were recited. Then the government took a hand in this affair and it was brought to court. As a result, St. Paul was compelled to leave the city. The Temple of Artemis was an architectural masterpiece which attracted people from all over the world for at least one thousand years as a holy place for pilgrimage. The most skilful architects and artists fashioned it.

*The Artemis Temple*

# ST. JOHN

Two important figures in the Christian religion, that is, St. Paul and St. John, lived in Ephesus. The former spent about five or six years trying to preach and proclaim this new religion in his workshop in Ephesus. The latter spent the last years of his century-long life here, wrote part of the New Testament and also died here. His tomb is on Ayasuluk hill. The church constructed by Emperor Justinian over this grave on the same hill, was one of the magnificent monuments of the Middle Ages.

When Jesus was crucified amidst the howls and laughter of the Jerusalem mob, St. John and Jesus' mother were nearby. On the Cross, He managed to adress St. John. Pointing to His mother He said "She is your mother, John", and to His mother He said "This is your son mother"; thereupon the disciple of Christ gladly undertook the responsibility to the end. After the crucifixion of Jesus, a kind of uneasiness spread among the people. Furthermore, when the brother of St. John and the son of Jesus' uncle were murdered, St. John realized that he could no longer live in this city smelling of blood. We have no information about St. John between the years 39 and 48 A.D., when the other followers of Christ were wandering and preaching this new religion. This hiatus of eleven years is perhaps indirect evidence of his stay in Ephesus.

In the first half of the 6th century A.D., Emperor Justinian ordered a basilica to be built over the tomb of St. John. It is on the eastern side of the Temple of Artemis, on a hill called Ayasuluk. After this building, the city which was constructed by Lysimachos, gradually moved to the foot of Ayasuluk hill, partly because of the unhealthy climate at the original site and partly for economic reasons. At last, in the 10th century, the city of Ephesus was completely settled around the hill.

*General View of church of St. John*

# THE CHURCH OF ST. JOHN

St. John came to Ephesus, lived here and wrote the fourth book of the New Testament, and died here. He himself compiled the fourth book in this old church. This church existed before the Seljuk Turks came. By means of finds from the excavations here, most of which were smuggled to Greece, Austria and other countries, it is now known that there were five small graves around the tomb of St. John. It is supposed that upon the wish of St. John, the other graves formed the shape of a cross with his tomb. From the very beginning of Christianity, the Christian communities accepted this place as a place of pilgrimage and paid homage here. Later on, this church was destroyed by acts of God and was built again, larger than the old one, by Emperor Justinian. This domed church had a fine courtyard surrounded with pillars. It was 110 m. in length, consisted of two storeys, and had six large and five small domes. The domes were covered with frescos and mosaics. During excavations, some coins were found belonging to the second half of the first century A.D. This indicates that the tomb of St. John used to be visited by people at that time. Holy wells, the places in which hymns were sung, and ashes which cured every kind of illness, were under the roof of these domes. The healing water flowing near the tomb of St. John had a special value for the pilgrims of that period. For about four or five years, St. John lived together with his rival Artemis! Though the Temple of Artemis was plundered more often than not, nobody touched St. John's church, because he was the great messenger of humanity, and disciple of Christ. "His tomb, just like the Church of St. Mary on the hill, was erected to suit a disciple. His memory will never be neglected by the western believers of the faith."

Though the Turks captured Ephesus in the early years of the 11th century, the Byzantines didn't leave the area until the beginning of the 14th century. The city was conquered by Isa Bey of the Menteşeoğulları Dynasty of that century (Isa Bey Mosque, a monumental witness to that period, can be seen on the plan). Later, the city became the capital of the Aydınoğulları Dynasty in the year 1348 A.D. After that, it was invaded by the Ottomans in the year 1390. The city lost its importance, or rather İzmir (Smyrna) became more important. The name of Ayasuluk was changed into Selçuk in the year 1914. The population of the city was 1.000, fifty years ago, but now it has reached 18,000.

*The Church of St. John*

## ST. MARY
## (THE VIRGIN MARY)

A sentence from the communiqué declared by the Third Council which met in Constantinople to the inhabitants says: "Cum in Ephesiorum civitatem pervenisest, in qua Yoannes Theologus et daipera Vergo Sancta Maria!" ("At the arrival of theologians John and the Holy Mother of God!"). The details of the life and death of St. Mary are not known, notwithstanding the two friends of St. Mary, that is, St. Luke and St. John, who do not leave us in the dark, but each of them talked about St. Mary differently. St. Luke in his book in the Bible, described St. Mary as a person who looked to the future with hope. These disciples, especially St. Paul, believing in Christ, furthered the expansion of the young religion and ensured its success. St. Luke related the life of Jesus' mother till the period of His ascension.

On the other hand, St. John looked at the matter from a different angle. He thought the beginning of a new age and the birth of this new creed was very agonizing, but in spite of all the dangers of violence, punishment and death, the new doctrine spread quickly. In the middle of all these was Mary, Jesus' mother, looking at the blood streaming from the wounds of the crucified Christ on the Cross. This was the holy birth of a new community. St. Mary was adored by Christ and the Church, but suffered greatly from pain and grief. She ran away to the desert. There God prepared a shelter for her to be fed. St. John wrote about Jesus mother being handed over to him in this way. St. John knew everything related to St. Mary and never left her alone, but always stayed with her. Especially after her son was crucified, it was not possible for the mother of Jesus to go on living in Jerusalem. She escaped from the inhabitants of that city, which worried the Christians in general. On the other hand, there is a peaceful quiet valley covered with forests, over by Panaya-Kapulu (the mountain on which St. Mary's House stands) near the city of Ephesus, in which she lived, so she found peace in this refuge. When people climb up the Solmissos mountain in order to celebrate Artemis in the "mystery" processions once a year, they aren't aware of the hidden St. Mary who is in fact the real person to be visited. Furthermore, there is a strong supposition that St. Paul knew St. Mary used to dwell in Ephesus. In the newly issued article with the title of "Schweizerische Kirchenzeitung", writting by Mr. F. Stricher, he declares "Pay your tribute to your dedicator St. Mary in Ephesus, not to Rome."

## THE CHURCH OF ST. MARY IN EPHESUS

The first three centuries kept the secret of St. Mary's misfortune and death, but perhaps it was God's will. The ancient world never realized the personality of the Virgin Mary. The city of Ephesus however, was fully conscious of paying honour to her. The first Christian church of Ephesus was built with columns in a classical style in the middle of a large open space, puzzling the people with its apperance and really deserving of its fame. No visitor to Ephesus neglects to visit the remains of the Church of St. Mary, which is very interesting not only from the spiritual point of view, but also for its architecture. Some of the old guides tell about a double church, but this is not certain. The old church building was altered three times with the changing fortunes of the city. The classical church was 260 m. in length, and was built with columns in the form of a fine basilica with baptistry. The Council and later on the Synod, declared this as the centre of Christianity in the year 449 A.D. After it was partly destroyed, the western part formed a domed basilica, and when this too was ruined, the eastern part of the old basilica was turned into a church. The baptistry of this church is the best preserved in Asia Minor. Ephesus made many friends owing to St. Mary. It is very interesting from the point of history, archaeology

*The Church of St. Mary*

and religion. "It reminds us of great Christian leaders like St. John, St. Timotheus, and especially St. Mary who lived a life of meditation, and further, it brings Christianity into the mind of the modern believer. The small modest convent of St. Mary over Panaya-Kapulu mountain, is the most beautiful natural residence imaginable. We feel indebted to write our thanks to all Turks, who showed a very refined and close concern for the subject."

# PANAYA-KAPULU or THE HOUSE OF VIRGIN MARY AT EPHESUS

For many years there have been two postu-

lates put forward concerning the death and the tomb of St. Mary, among Christian communities.

1. As the historians declare, "dormitio Hietosoymitana" that is, "the death is in Jerusalem", at the place where Jesus was born, He was killed too"

2. Again some historians affirm: "dormito Ephesian" that is, "the death is in Ephesus", so that this divine death took place in the presence of the disciple St. John, in whose care Christ's mother was given in Ephesus. (St. John, XX, 26-27) According to the Latins, St. John mentioned in his writings that he lived together with his successor in his home. Therefore he must have lived in Ephesus, must have become a bishop there, and died there. His grave, over which Justinian ordered a colossal basilica

to be erected, is still there. Meanwhile, that era of Ephesus had a strong historical background continuing up to the 7th century. Famous writes of old, like Cornelius, Lapide, Serry, Tillement, Baillet and Benoit, etc. were its defenders. The Pope issued a communiqué as follows between the years 1740-58: "St. John has performed his alotted duty perfectly well".

On his leaving for Ephesus he took Mary with him, and there the Holy Mother ascended to Heaven. Many of the theologians proclaim in their writings that St. Mary lived in Ephesus.

Lipsius accepts for certain that the Virgin Mary followed St. John to the city of Ephesus (Ses Actes Apotres Apocryhès, Brunswick, 1883, P. 448). The theologian Ernst Gurtius, goes further: "The tomb of the Virgin Mary was in Ephesus in the 1st century A.D." He gave this report in the presence of a group of gentlemen who had come together for a discussion about Ephesus on 7th March 1874, Berlin. A lot can be written about Mary's death and her tomb in Ephesus. The first formal worship of Christianity, and the first church and basilica constructed in honour of St. Mary, arose in Ephesus. The spiritual council was held here among the magnificent ruins for the first time. For many years, on the fifteenth of August in every year, the Easter of Panaya-Kapulu has been celebrated near the Holy Fountain. Catherine Emmerich, a Bavarian woman, maintained one Easter that the Virgin Mary had definitely died in Ephesus and not in Jerusalem, and the last remains of the tomb could be seen in the earth, not further than 500 m. from the present building. Emmerich said that one could see the Aegean Sea and the smooth road leading to the Church of St. Mary, from the hill on which the house of St. Mary stood. This was a wonderful revelation and

*View of the Interior of the House of St. Mary*

was uttered between the years 1822-24. In 1982, Mr. M. Poulain and Mr. Young, who were interested in the Ephesus question, wanted to investigate the prediction of the pious woman from Bavaria, on the spot. Starting from Bulbul mountain, they looked for the places mentioned by this woman, who had no education and never went out of the country of her birth. The researchers did not know which direction to take. There was indeed not even a path over the mountain. They searched every where carefully among the thickets. At last, at the end of the third day, they explored the place the soothsayer woman had mentioned. They found the holy ash mentioned, in the fireplace of St. Mary's house on Panaya-Kapulu. Thus the holy house and the ruins became acknowledged in the Christian world.

Unfortunately, the grave of St. Mary which was proclaimed by Catherine Emmerich as being 500 m. from the house, was not discovered. The search for it proved a failure. The search for the grave requires serious and scientific research which should be done by archaeologists, together with an authoritative Christian theologian. This is not impossible. To unearth this grave would not only interest the Christian world, but also the Muslim people who have a deep respect for St. Mary.

In many Surahs (chapters of the Koran) St. Mary is mentioned, and it is accepted how miraculously she gave birth to Jesus. Muslims acknowledge Christ, therefore they have the deepest respect and reverence for His Holy Mother.

*The House of St. Mary*

# THE CHURCH OF ST. MARY

The building to the north of the Harbour Gymnasium, was turned into a church and dedicated to St. Mary, and it was then called by this name after Emperor Constantine decreed that Christianity be made a lawful religion in the year 313 A.D. The length of the first basilica was 260 m., and it was adapted into a church. Formerly, this building had been a clearing-house called Deigma. 111 general consuls with 200 bishops, gathered together in this building for the first time and proclaimed a communiqué for the birth of Christianity in the year 431 A.D. According to them, St. Mary was the Mother of God. Pope Paul VI prayed in front of the Cross seen in the picture, on the 26th of July in the year 1967. The sentence in memory of this visit, written in Latin on the plate under the Cross, is as follows: "Summus pontifex Paulus Sextus in hac sacra aede preces effudis die XXVI Juliannic MCMLX."

*The Church of St. Mary*

*The Gate of Pursuit*

## THE GATE OF PURSUIT

The entrance to the inner citadel of Selçuk. The castle of Ayasuluk is situated on a hill to the right of the Izmir-Ephesus highway, the gate being on the southern tip of the slope. It was built in the 7-8 centuries during reinforcements made to the fortress walls to withstand Arab attacks, and is flanked by two high towers. The gate itself is arched and leads into a small enclosed courtyard in which the entrapped enemy could be slaughtered by those defending the fortress should they breach the main gate. It is one of the most recent courtyard gates of this kind in Anatolia.

## AYASULUK FORTRESS

The Inner and Outer Keep: The Ayasuluk fortress, site of the church of St. John, was a Roman necropolis It became a citadel housing the inhabitants of the surrounding area when Ephesus had ceased to be a major mercantile centre in the 5th century A.D. The walls date from that period, when the citadel was also reinforced by an inner keep surrounding the summit of the hill. The outer fortifications are pierced by three gates to the east, west and south. The fortifications were repeatedly repaired up to the Middle Ages. Within them lies the tomb of St. John, buried here at his own request, over which, in the 4th century, a small basilical church was built, later to be replaced during the reign of the emperor Justinian by the present church of St. John. It stands opposite the fabled temple of Artemis, one of the seven wonders of the ancient world, with which it vies in grandeur. With the arrival of the Turks in the region, a third splendid monument, the Isabey mosque, was erected between them in 1375

*General view of the Church of St. John and of the Fortress*

17

*Tomb of St. John*

# CHURCH OF ST. JOHN

The church is 130 m. in length, cruciform in plan and fronted by an atrium to the west, leading into a narthex. The church itself is threenaved, the tomb of St. John situated before the apse in the central nave. The six domes of the church are supported along its length by massive piers running between the naves, flanked by two storeys of blue and grey-veined columns. Capitals of the lower row of columns bear the monograms of the emperor Justinian and empress Theodora. A narrow flight of steps leads to the crypt from before the apse where there is also a small, narrow horizontal window. Medieval legend claimed that a curative vapour emitted from that window turned the church into a centre of pilgrimage. The mosaics over the crypt were later restored.

# CHAPEL WITH FRESCOES

This is a small, wooden roofed chapel to the north of the crypt, dating from the 10th century. A well preserved fresco may still be seen above the pool-like apse, showing the figure of Christ flanked on the right by a saint and on the left by St. John himself. Immediately flanking the church is the clergical treasure house, an octagonal, two storeyed building.

*Chapel with Frescoes*

*The Isabey Mosque*

## ISA BEY MOSQUE

When you look to the west over Ayasuluk hill, you face the view in the picture. The mosque was erected in 1375 by Isa Bey, the son of Mehmet Bey from the Aydınoğulları dynasty, a dynasty of the Seljuks. One third of the structure is the covered part of the mosque, and two thirds of it is the courtyard, all of which were built on a plot 57 m. long by 51 m. wide. You can enter the inner courtyard, the cupola of which was destroyed, through the western gate. You can go into the real mosque building through a portal with three arches. Two of the cupolas on the black granite pillars and arches are ornamented with milk-white and dark blue porcelain tiles. As in all the other structures of this kind in the area, the material used in this building was brought from Ephesus. The granite columns and their capitals were transported from the Harbour Baths. One of the minarets still stands.

## THE FACADE OF ISA BEY MOSQUE

This mosque which was built by the son of Mushmish from Damascus, is one of the most beautiful examples of Islamic architecture. The actual facade is the side where its minaret stands. The windows and the door are embellished with rich ornamentation. In the earlier building there were wooden arches upholding the two sides of the domes.

# THE TEMPLE OF ARTEMIS (Diana)

If you walk two or three hundred metres from Ephesus Museum on the right-hand side of the road leading to Ephesus and Kuşadası from Selçuk, towards Isa Bey Mosque, you will come across a large hole. As you can see in the picture, over this large hole, which turns into a pool of water in the spring months, the Temple of Artemis once used to stand. It played an important part in the social and religious life of Ephesus. The first builders of the temple were said to be the Amazons. Plinius the writer, reports that the temple was ransacked seven times in its history. When Ephesus came under the rule of Croesus, the King of the Lydians, he saw that the Ephesians had Kersifron, the architect from Crete, and his son Metagenes, to rebuild the temple. He himself donated pillars, the lower parts of which were decorated with reliefs. This temple of the Archaic period was burned by a madman named Herostratos in the year 356 A.D. two hundred years after its construction. Then the temple, which was one of the 7 Wonders of the World, was re-built to the same measurements as the old temple, that is 425 feet in length, 220 feet in width and 60 feet in height, and decorated with 120 pillars in the Ionian style. From here, you can see Ayasuluk on which Isa Bey Mosque and the Church of St. John stand. In the distance behind them the Byzantine castle can be seen. The temple was maintained up to the year 111 A.D., but it was torn down and pillaged by the Goths in 263 A.D. It was not erected again because Christianity had won its victory, pagan temples had been torn down or re-adapted. After this demolition, most of the marble pillars were carried to Istanbul to be used in the construction of Hagia Sophia. The spark emitted by this demolition kindled the torch of culture in Ephesus, which will shed light on history forever. The rare finds of the temple were, the first time, found by English archaeologists in the middle of the 19th century after long research and excavation. Most of the remnants which have architectural value, and belonged to the Temple of Artemis, are now in the British Museum. Some of them, made of gold and ivory, are in the Archaeology Museum in Istanbul and in the Ephesus museum.

*General view of the Temple of Artemis*

*The Beautiful Artemis*

# THE STADIUM

It occupies an area of 229 m. by 295 m. It is the space between the arches on the left and the gate on the right. Different sports contests such as horse-racing, and chariot-racing were performed here. There was a round arena on the east side where gladiators fought. The covered arches on the left side along the stadium were made for keeping the animals brought from hot countries. There were stone steps on the slope seen on the right, on which spectators sat. The seating places, were formed by filling the spaces with soil.

*The Stadium*

# STADIUM GATEWAY

The stadium was built in the time of Emperor Nero in the first century A.D. (54 - 58). It is a work of architecture belonging to the Roman period. The gate seen in the picture is supposed to have been constructed in the 3rd or 4th century A.D. It is reckoned that the stadium had a capacity for 13.000 spectators. The stone steps of the stadium which were used as seats, no longer exist, having been carried to Ayasuluk hill in order to build the structures there.

*Stadium Gateway*

*The Harbour Baths*

## THE HARBOUR BATHS

You come across the remnants of these buildings constructed with huge stones and gracefully carved marble, between the Double Churches and the Harbour Street. These baths in the south, 200 m. from the churches, belong to the Roman period of the 2nd century A.D. Emperor Constantine restored them in the 4th century and they were named after him. You can see some pedestals on which many precious statues once used to stand in the large salon in the picture. There was a covered swimming pool to the north of this salon. Magnificent granite pillars which once used to decorate this swimming pool, now support the domes of Isa Bey Mosque. The excavations at this spot did not reveal the warm - water (tepidarium), and the hot - water (caldarium) parts of the baths. Again it is said that a valuable bronze statue was dug out in the excavation of 1926, and carried away to the Museum of Vienna.

## A PIECE OF ARCHTRAVE

This is the moulding of the exterior of an arch or a part surrounding the doorway of the Harbour Baths.

# POOL FROM THE HARBOUR BATHS

One enters the courtyard of the harbour baths from the main harbour road. The court is a colonnaded atrium which leads to the baths via a monumental portal, flanked on either side by rectangular pools with bulls head and garland relief carving to either side.

*The Harbour Baths*

# THE HARBOUR (ARCADIAN) STREET

This street led to the harbour from the Great Theatre and was lined with columns along each side for its length of 530 m. Its width is 21 m. This street, which was the most important one of the city, was restored by Emperor Arcadius (395 - 408 A.D.). so that it was called Arcadian after him. The middle section is paved with marble and is 11 m. wide; both pillared side sections of the street are 5 m. wide each. According to the knowledge acquired through excavations, the street, decorated with statues, was illuminated by candle-like street lamps at night. There was a Harbour Gate at the place where the street came to the sea. This gate still stands there in its elegance but photos can't be taken of it because of the marshy land around. There was a sewage system under the street. In the distance on the horizon, you can discern the hill over which St. Paulus was put into pri-

*The Harbour Street*

son and for this reason it is called the Prison of St. Paulus.

Four monumental columns thought to date to the 4th century are to be found in the centre of the harbour road. Although it is not known why these were originally erected, they are thought to have born the statues of the four authors of the New Testament.

*View of the Theatre from the Harbour Street*

# COMMERCIAL AGORA

A stoa to the right of the marble road leading away from the theatre was uncovered, dating to the reign of the emperor Nero. restoration of this building is still underway. The stoa fronts the agora of Ephesus. This has three monumental gates, the northern, western and southern gates, flanking the Celsus Library. The southern gate has been restored. The stoa contained a single row of shops of standard dimensions fronted by a row of columns. In the centre of the court stood a water clock, which has been removed to the eastern gallery for restoration. Originally built in the Hellenistic period, the agora underwent considerable changes during the reign of Augustus.

## THE GREAT THEATRE OF THE CITY

This theatre framed by three walls on the left, right and in the front, is at the western foot of Panayır mountain at the beginning of Harbour Street The stage building, which is very valuable from the art historical point of view, is one of the best preserved contructions in Ephesus up to the present moment. It had three storeys; the second storey, decorated with pillars, statues and graceful carvings, was built by Nero in the first century, and the third storey was built by Septimus Severus at the end of the 2nd century A.D.

*The Great Theatre*

## MONUMENTAL THEATRE ORCHESTRA

Semi circular area between the auditorium and the skene in which classical choruses stood in one or two rows, chanting out their lines in unison. The orchestra of the theatre of Ephesus is particularly well-preserved. During excavations here traces were also found of a Hellenistic theatre.

# THE GREAT THEATRE

This has been unearthed year by year continuously. The last building alterations were made by Emperor Claudius (41-54 A.D.) and Emperor Trajanus (98-117 A.D.). It had a capacity of 25.000 spectators, with 22 flights of stairs, each set by three circular rows. The theatre has a diameter of 50 m. A street on the upper side of the theatre leads to Curetes Street. Most of the stone stair seats were carried away to be used in other constructions.

This monumental masterpiece of Ephesus is important not only from the point of view of art, but also from the point of the conflict between Christianity and idolatry. In the early years of Christianity, one of the big combats between the followers of Artemis and of Christ had taken place in this theatre, and as a result, St. Paulus was put into the prison on the hill named after him, and he was then obliged to leave Ephesus.

*The Great Theatre*

*The Great Theatre*

*The Great Theatre*

## MAZEUS AND MITHRIADATES GATE

This picture shows one of the two inscriptions inscribed in Greek and Latin on the marble between the south of the Agora and the Library. These tablets were the front part of a colossal portal erected by two slaves in order to render their indebtness to Emperor Augustus, Empress Liviae, and their daughter Julia and son-in-law Agruppa, who had forgiven them and bestowed their freedom upon them. Let us pass through the relics of this portal, 16 m. in height, which has four niches. Parts above these inscriptions were embellished with bronze and golden covers.

*Mazeus and Mithriadates Gate*

# THE LIBRARY OF CELSUS

C. Julius had this library built in honour of his father C. Celsus, the General Governor of the Province of Asia, in the year 135 A.D. You climb up to the salon of the library by nine stairs. Here, there used to be four statues symbolizing Justice. Virtue, etc. The niches in the walls were used for books. In front of the niches there were low Ionian pillars, made into the shape of a table. The inscription at the nothern end of the library in Latin, and another inscription at the southern end in Greek, are about Celsus and his son, Aquila. The grave of Celsus is at the back. You can go to the grave after you climb down the stairs on the right-hand side, passing through a winding narrow corridor of 15 m. You will see a beautiful sarcophagus made of white marble, with a length of 2.5 m. The face of this sarcophagus is adorned with sculptures of snakes together with sculptures of Eros. Nike and Medusa. Under the stairs leading to Marble Street, is a newly discovered sarcophagus belonging to the Byzantine period. A lead plate at the bottom, on which the corpse lay, was found.

*The Library of Celsus (Beginning of 2nd Cent. AD)*

The Library of Celsus (Beginning of 2nd Cent. AD)

## THE MARBLE STREET

This is the main street of the city; it has a remarkable sewer. The street leads to the Koressos Gate in the north, and to the Magnesia Gate in the south, and from there it leads to the Seven Sleepers and the Temple of Artemis. There were columns 8 m. high, on which graceful marbles were sculpted with friezes, along the left side of the Marble Street, for its length of 4 km, as seen in the picture.

*The Marble Street, the Library of Celsus and the Agora*

# THE SERAPIS TEMPLE

This was built in dedication to Serapis, one of the Egyptian gods, in the 2nd century A.D. Its facade once reached up to 29 m. including the pedestals and capitals. Three columns out of a total of eight were really colossal, that is, they were 15 m. high and weighed 50 tons. Each one was ornamented with three Corinthian capitals made from one block of marble. The fragments of these columns and their capitals can be seen in the picture. One could enter a salon from the street in the market place; this salon was encircled by columns. One could go into the small salon from a large one by means of 12 steps.

*The Serapis Temple*

*Latrina (Public Toilets)*

## FOOTPRINT CARVED INTO THE PAVEMENT TO SHOW THE WAY TO THE BROTHEL

On Marble Street, a footprint was carved to show the way to the Brothel. This footprint and the sign near the middle of the street towards the Great Theatre, direct the way to the brothel.

# THE BROTHEL

The house you see in the picture is the brothel. It is at the end of the Marble Street on the left. It dates from the 4th century. A.D. careful health control dominated the brothel, even more than in today's brothels. The men coming to the house, first washed and cleaned their hands and feet before entering a large salon through a hallway. This house, which had every kind of facility for cleanliness, was dedicated to Venus, therefore, statuettes of Venus (Aphrodite) used to stand in the salon, the inside of which was covered with marble.

*The Brothel*

# THE BATH OF SKOLASTICIA

The upper part of this bath, which formed a salon and had central heating, is ruined. There was a swimming pool, having a hot bath (caldarium), a warm bath (tepidarium), a cold bath (frigidarium) and a dressing room (apodyterium). Though the first building of this bath, which had three floors, belonged to the 2nd century, a woman named Skolasticia adapted it into the present condition, making it available to hundreds of people in the 4th century. There were not only public rooms, but also private rooms. Those who wished could stay here for many days. The furnace and the large boiler of the heating system which provided heat and hot water for the salon, the rooms, and for a very large bath, were on the first floor. Only a massive arch of the third floor is left.

*Caldarium of the Bath of Skolasticia*

# THE STATUE OF SKOLASTICIA

This is the statue of the woman who had the baths built in Ephesus in such a magnificent way that nobody could help admiring them. Just near this statue was the entrance gate with its five stairs to the road leading to the Great Theatre.

*Statue of Skolasticia, who restored the Bath (4th Cent. AD)*

# CURETES STREET

Lysimachos, who rebuilt the city, resto-red this street, which was regarded as sacred, preserving its original shape, in 290 B.C.

*Curetes Street*

## CURETES STREET AND THE TEMPLE OF HADRIAN

After Theodosius restored the temple seen on the left in 391 A.D., he opened it to the public in honour of his father, General Theodosius, who was hanged innocently. The ruins just in front of the temple were houses for the rich, and boarding houses, which have been unearthed recently in Ephesus.

*The Temple of Hadrian*

## CURETES STREET

There is a rise in the street offering a pleasant view before it arrives at the meeting point of the hills. The headless statue on the right was erected in honour of a woman doctor who did great service to her country; it belongs to the Byzantine period. A statue of Memmius, grandson of the dictator Sulla of the Roman Empire, used to stand on the road leading to the south. In front of the above mentioned statue there was a spring of water called HYDREION

*Curetes Street*

# THE FOUNTAIN OF TRAJAN

After the Temple of Hadrian, on the way up the foot of Panayır mountain, this is the second building restored on the left. This fountain, 12 m. high, had two storeys. The first storey was 7 m. high and the second storey 5 m. high. Twelve statues of Venus, Starun, Dionysos and the successors of the Imperial Family, were discovered here. The fountain was erected in dedication to Emperor Trajan in the 1st century A.D.

*The Fountain of Trajan*

# NIKE, THE GODDESS OF VICTORY

You can see a relief of Nike, the winged goddes of victory. She holds a wreath made from laurel leaves, an emblem of victory, in her left hand, and a stalk of wheat in her right hand; she is in a flying position. This comes from the Roman period and was discovered among the ruins on the Square of Domitian.

*The Relief of Nike*

*The Fountain of Pollio*

# THE FOUNTAIN OF POLLIO
# (Early 1st Century A.D.)

It was constructed by the Temple of Domitian in dedication to C. SEXTILLIUS by Offilius Proculus in the first century A.D. There used to be a space covered with marble slabs and decorated with statues in front of this fountain. One of those statues, the statue of a warrior in a resting position, is in the Museum of Ephesus now.

45

# HERACLES

You pass through the carved columns in the picture if you don't keep walking along Curetes Street toward the Temple of Domitian, but take the direction towards the Palace of the Municipality.

## THE MEMORIAL TO MEMMIUS

This is one of the monuments decorating the Square of Domitian. It was erected in the 1st century in honour of Memmius, the grandson of the dictator Sulla. At the end of the same century a fountain was added in front. The memorial was decorated with various carvings.

## THE TEMPLE OF DOMITIAN

This structure is the first one along the continuation of Marble Street. This two-floored building contained the warehouses and shops on the first floor, and the temple on the second floor. It was built in dedication to Emperor Domitian.

*General view of the Houses on the Slope*

*The Side view of the Peristyl House*

# A PERISTYLE HOUSE

This was unearthed in the excavations of the fifth terrace in 1969. The atrium (ie. central court of the Roman house) with a pool of water in the middle, was sorruonded by rooms ornamented with frescoes and mosaics. There is also a mosaic with exquisite figures on the floor. The walls of the atrium are covered with marble up to a certain level. The house was used for three or four centuries beginning in the 1st century A.D.

*Peristyl House B2 (View from the north east)*

*Houses on the Slope (Plan of the B House)*

*Theatre Room, the upper panel of the north wall. It shows the fight between Heracles and Akhelos*

*South wall of the Theatre Room. A woman frescoe holding a pearl string*

North wall of the Theatre room. A woman frescoe with a diadem

# THE PALACE OF THE COUNCIL

A lot of excavations have been made to explore this monument. Many inscribed slabs and statues of Diana, beside the fine pillars, as seen in the picture, were unearthed. There were rooms around a sacrifical pool in the middle. The upper part of the construction belongs to the Roman period, the lower part belongs to the Hellenistic period. It is conjectured that, it was constructed by Emperor Augustus in the 1st or 2nd century A.D. There was a front garden at the palace. People used to enter a second garden, built in the Doric style, through the front garden. This was the palace used for organising city affairs, and it was also the dwelling place of the governmental body of the province. The pillars seen in the picture (which were four in number), were the projections of the roof of the salon over which the sacred fire once burned continuously.

*The Palace of the Council*

*The Palace of the Council (Prytaneion)*

## THE PALACE OF THE COUNCIL (PRYTANEION)

Two temples were discovered during excavations to the east of the palace. These temples disappeared under the buildings constructed by the Byzantines. Three statues of Artemis, now in the Museum of Ephesus, were found in the place seen in the picture. When the statues of Artemis decorated with statuettes were being unearthed in 1956, it was supposed that those statues were hidden in this place for preservation.

*The Varius Baths*

## THE VARIUS BATHS

It is supposed that these were constructed as a gymnasium. The hot water section (caldarium) was unearthed near the big rock on the slope. There were also a frigidarium, tepidarium, resting rooms, reading rooms and sitting rooms in the baths. They were built in the 2nd century but were restored, and new rooms were added in later years.

# ODEON
## (Small theatre, or concert hall)
## Bouleuterion

This was constructed by Vedius Antonius and his wife in the 2nd century A.D. and was a small salon for plays and concerts seating an audience of 1,500 people. This theatre had 22 stairs conforming to the shape of the theatre as seen in the picture. The upper part of the theatre was decorated with red granite pillars in the Corinthian style. The entrances were at both sides of the stage and reached by a few steps. It is speculated that the theatre was once covered over, because there was no drainage system.

*Odeion-Bouleuterion*

# THE CAVES OF THE SEVEN SLEEPERS (ESHAB ÜL-KEHF)

This is the place where seven Christian young men hid themselves with their dog when they were fleeing the wrath and punisment of the idolators. Later, they were found and murdered during the reign of Decius, the Roman emperor, in the middle of the 3rd century. It is said that they were ressurected after 200 years during the reign of Emperor Theodosius II in the 5th century. After that resurrection, many of those who believed in Christ wished to be buried in this place and they were, so that a large graveyard was formed with about a thousand graves, tombs and monasteries. Up to the 6th century it was enlarged continually and became a place of pilgrimage. This continued up to the 12th century. After that century it fell into ruins. The graves are on the slope of Panayır mountain facing Selçuk. The legend told above does not only exist in Christianity, but is also known as "Eshab Ül-Kehf" in the Muslim world.

## THE STATUE OF SAINT MARY IN THE OLIVE GROVE

You can climb up Panaya-Kapulu by a smooth but winding asphalt road, 9 km. in length, from Ephesus. After climbing up the hill 450 m. high above sea-level, you come down again a hundred metres over a slope, until you arrive at a peaceful place, where there are some inhabitants, and buildings that create an air of holiness. Let us walk to the left side. When you pass through the olive trees, the first significant thing to be seen is the statue of St. Mary on the wall under the trees, which welcomes you with raised arms. Hundreds of people regarded as pilgrims, pass before this statue with reverence on every day of the year, especially at Easter. You can come here on foot from the shore.

*Cistern*

# THE HOUSE OF ST. MARY

As you see in the picture, religious ceremonies are often held here, and the place is treated with reverence and respect. Pope Benoit said, "St. John who came to Ephesus, brought St. Mary with him and this happiest Mother ascended to heaven here!"

# THE HOUSE OF ST. MARY

The view of St. Mary's House after restoration. The house was discovered through the explorations of Père Poulin and Young in the year 1892, and formerly its site was predicted by the Bavarian sage, Catherine Emmerich (1774-1824), two years before her death. When the house was discovered, the roof was broken down and only the ruins of the walls were left standing. It is said that those were the ruins of a church dedicated to St. Mary in the 9th century.

*The House of St. Mary*

# VIEW OF THE INTERIOR OF ST. MARY'S HOUSE

You enter this part through the little door shown in the other picture after passing through a small salon. Pope Leon XII, Peter X, Leon XII in 1903 and many others, thought that St. Mary lived in Ephesus. They decided in the year 1914, that this place, called Panghia Capulu, was sacred and should be visited by pilgrims. After visiting St. Mary, do not turn back please, walk forward a little and come down the slope.

*View of the Interior of St. Mary's House*

# THE FOUNTAIN OF ST. MARY

St. Mary lived her last days drinking the healing water of this fountain (30-35 A.D.). There are so many miracles worked by this water and by the ash in the fireplace of St. Mary's House, that there is hardly anybody who has not witnessed them; people with cancer, whom doctors said were incurable, cripples brought on a stretcher, and children with disabled bones from birth, have all been cured here.

*The Fountain of St. Mary*

## SMALL ARTEMIS
(or LA BELLE ARTEMIS) OF
EPHESUS

Though this goddess has the same name as the sister of the Greek god Apollo, the god of the sun, it is clear that they have different characteristics. The goddess at Ephesus was the goddess of nature and of animals, and particularly she is the mother and protector of young girls. According to the information provided, Artemis is identified with her two animals. This statue was discovered in one of the large salons of the Palace of the Council, half-buried in the earth. The upper part of the statue from the stomach is coverd with gold. It is possible to see a truly divine expression on the face. Unfortunately, the baton which was in her hand has remained undiscovered. Above the waist are a lot of eggs symbolizing fertility and abundance; her necklace is embellished with signs of the Zodiac, and over them, decorations. The lower part of the statue is ornamented with mythical animals.

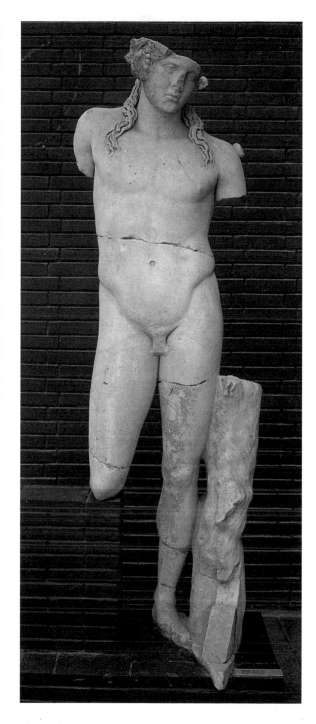

## THE ROMAN SARCOPHAGUS

As seen in the picture, the figures of Eros and Nike with heads of the medusa and two portraits of the owners of the sarcophagus, are all delicately wrought among the knot-work on the sides of the sarcophagus. One part of the lid has been broken.

## THE STATUE OF DIONYSOS

This was one of the statues decorating the Fountain of Trajan. It is a Roman copy of the statue made at the beginning of the 2nd century. You can see a cluster of grapes in the hair.

## EROS AND THE DOLPHIN

This was discovered near the Fountain of Trajan (2nd century A.D.). It is sculpted from bronze and was used as a fountain. It shows Eros mounted on a dolphin. It is only one of the exquisite creations of art to be seen in the Museum of Ephesus.

## PRIAPOS OR GOD BES

Found during excavations of the brothel, a figurine of baked clay which is the notorius phallic symbol of Ephesus.

## HEAD OF EROS

This was found in the vicinity of the Odeon. It is carved in marble and is a Roman copy of the bronze statue of Eros with a stretched bow, made by a famous sculptor, M. Lysippos. The other parts of the statue have not been discovered. The head is now in the Museum of Ephesus.

## THE COLOSSAL STATUE OF ARTEMIS

It shows the special characteristics of Artemis of Ephesus. It was made larger than the other Artemis statue and there is a huge crown on the head (1st century B.C.). It was discovered in the Palace of the Council and has been preserved without much deterioration.

The statues of Artemis were found in the excavations carried out during the last century. They are all in the Museum of Ephesus. In the picture, you see the largest Artemis of all. The designs carved on this masterpiece bear no relation to ancient Greek art, and suggest that the earlier idea of Artemis was derived from the East. There are small-sized animal figures from the tables: bees, lambs, the heads of lions, crabs, deer and bulls carved in high relief on the statue, which wears a slender drapery ornamented with the abovementioned figures.

*The Fresco of Socrates*

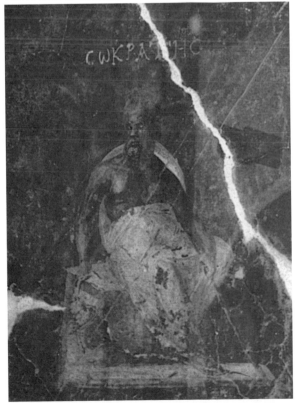

*The Colossal Statue of Artemis*

## THE FRESCO OF SOCRATES

This was discovered in the room of Socrates in the Palace on the Slope in Ephesus. The philosopher was sculpted in a sitting position with a baton in his hand. On the lower section his name was inscribed.

*Statue of a warrior*

## STATUE OF A WARRIOR

This was discovered near the Fountain of Pollio in front of the Temple of Domitian. It was hewn in a resting position in front of the fountain. The Warrior had held a sword and shield in his left hand and he used to hold something in his right hand. Though the statue has been largely broken, it has a lively expression on its face and a slim body. It is now in the museum.

## SACRIFICIAL PLACE IN THE TEMPLE OF DOMITIAN

This was discovered in the Temple of Domitian in Ephesus. The marble slabs you see in the picture are only one part of the sacrificial place built in the 1st century A.D. The designs on them illustrate the ending of the battle and the sign of victory.

*Sacrificial Place in the Temple of Domitian*

## HEAD OF ZEUS

This is one of the works from a group of statues which were once used to decorate the Fountain of Pollio built in the 1st century B.C. It has been preserved in good condition, and a god-like expression on the face can be clearly seen.

*Markus Aurelius Bust-Marble (3 rd century A.D.)*

## HEAD OF SOCRATES

Though this is partly broken, it still reflects the facial expression of the philospher. It belongs to the Roman period and is exhibited in the museum.

## KUŞADASI

Kuşadası is called by this name because of the small island seen in front of it.

When one thinks of Kuşadası the sea comes to mind. It is a sea full of vigour and life. Man lives very close to nature here and feels rest in his soul. All the coastline of Kuşadası gives this impression. It is possible to see the scenery along the coast in nice weather for eight months of the year. The coast is 50 km. long, and has been embellished with different coloured tents looking like bunches of flowers. The sea is always blue here.